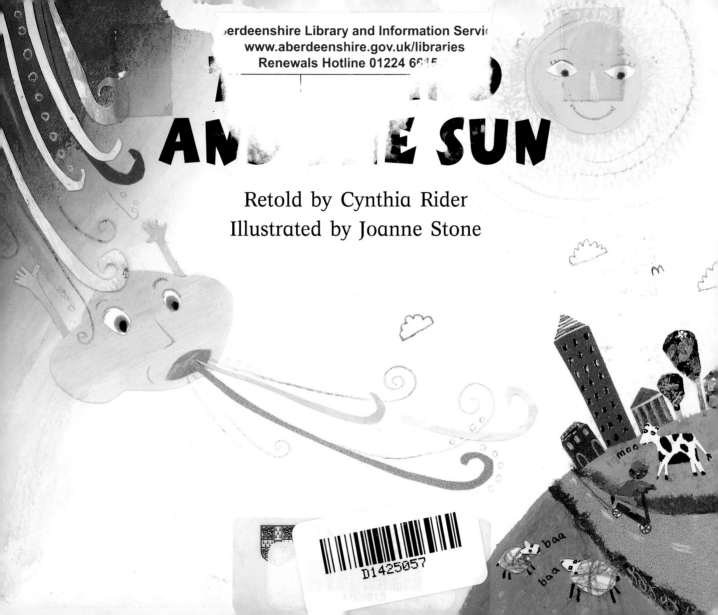

AN... ...E SUN

Retold by Cynthia Rider
Illustrated by Joanne Stone

"Look at me,"
cried the wind.
"I can zoom.
I can swoop.
I can loop the loop.
I am stronger than you."

"That's not true," said the sun. "I wake up the days with my golden rays. *I* am stronger than you."

3

You are not very strong

"No, no," said the wind.
"You are not very strong.
You just play in the sky.
You play all day long."

4

"I chase away the rain," said the sun, "and I make the sky blue. *I* can make big rainbows too."

"But I am *strong*,"
said the wind.
"I can make a tree sway.
I can blow a roof away.
People are afraid of *me*."

6

"Look down," said the sun.
"Can you see that boy
on a new blue scooter?
His name is Luke and
he's on his way to school.
The one who makes him
take his coat off is the strongest."

7

"I can soon do that," said the wind,
and he began to blow.
Whoosh!
All the trees began to sway.
Whoosh!
All the birds flew away.

8

"It's cold today,"
said Luke.
He did up
the buttons
on his coat,
to keep warm.

The wind came zooming
and swooping across the sky.
He blew Luke off
his new blue scooter.
But the wind could not
blow Luke's coat off.

10

Luke picked up his scooter,
and away he went
with a hoot and a toot.

11

The wind blew again . . .
and again.

"That coat must be stuck on
with glue," he said. "It's no use.
I can't make Luke take it off."

"I can make him take it off," said the sun.
"Just you wait and see!"

13

The sun grew hotter and
hotter, and so did Luke!
"Phew! It's hot," he said.
So . . . he took his coat off!

14

"Hooray! I made him do it!"
cried the sun.
   The wind looked gloomy.
   "It's not fair!" he said,
and he zoomed away.

15

The sun smiled.
"I am the strongest,"
he said.
"I always was,
and I always will be."

16